STILL
a Good
Thing

"Damaged BUT not UnDone"

LATARSHA MACK

All Scripture verses, unless otherwise indicated, are taken from the Holy Bible, the New King James Version®. Copyright © 1982 by Thomas Nelson. Used by permission. All rights reserved.

Scripture taken from The Message. Copyright © 1993, 1994, 1995, 1996, 2000, 2001, 2002. Used by permission of NavPress Publishing Group.

Scriptures marked AMP and AMPC are taken from the Amplified Bible (AMP) and Amplified Bible, Classic Edition: Scripture taken from the Amplified® Bible, Copyright © 1954, 1958, 1962, 1964, 1965, 1987 by the Lockman Foundation Used by Permission. (www.Lockman.org).

Holy *Bible*, New Living Translation, copyright © 1996, 2004, 2015 by Tyndale House Foundation. Used by permission of Tyndale House Publishers, Inc., Carol Stream, Illinois 60188. All rights reserved.

Dedication

This book is to inspire women who have and are going through the "Process" of many challenges that have pricked their vulnerability and challenged their confidence while defying not being a slave to the emotional rollercoaster of the many different phases of hurt, resentment and failure. It is to help identify who you are as a woman and to recognize your strength as an Army Strong Warrior that looks defeat straight in the eyes to bow down and then walk right through valleys of uncertainties, discomforts and shadows of death with confidence, while strategizing every step and move.

As you travel through my steps and my storm of divorce, I pray that you will be inspired to continue your walk in Christ and know that God does heal all wounds, even the ones you think are difficult to heal and overcome.

To my children Jamea, Jalil and Josiah you watched me Trust God during the most difficult times; a divorce, and you never gave up on me. You are my inspiration and each of you motivated me in your own

special way to push towards the mark of what God is calling me to. God knew I would have given up a long time ago if I did not have the will to fight, still in me, and if I did not have my children.

I thank my children for believing in me and always loving me. I thank God for supporting me during the good and the bad times. You are my *Jehovah-Jireh*; now I understand that you are more than enough for me.

Mom

Foreword

This book displays the prophetic characteristic given to new Author, LaTarsha Mack by God. In spite of her shattered dreams, broken-heart, betrayal, hurts, disappointments, and even ungodly selfish choices; there is **Still Greatness** in each of us.

Using the Master's key to unlock a measure of FAITH within us, God will ignite the HOPE of Glory to nullify areas in your life that you may have suppressed and hidden from people, but not erased from your mind, and often reminded by the cares of this World.

Her prophetic Anointing has given her the opportunity to embrace and activate spiritual principles in the lives of many, while deception and confusion has become normal.

LaTarsha Mack is transparent in her writing to expose her personal experiences in life, being relative to that of an EKG monitor of the heart; ups-and-downs.

She stands on the Word of God that says *"I can do all things through Christ who strengthens me."* — **Philippians 4:13.**

LaTarsha's compassion to see women from all walks of life that may have been Damaged; accept the Reality; "YOU ARE STILL GOOD."

As you read this book, let your mind be transformed through the *Revelation of GOD's LOVE*— 1Jn. 4:8-10—KJV.

VALIDATED BY GOD!!!

Apostle, Dr. John H. Chambers
Founder and Senior Pastor
Believers of Authority Ministries, Inc.

Endorsements

"Still A Good Thing," as given by the Holy Spirit to LaTarsha Mack is not just another literary work for reading. It is a revelation on how one can live life victoriously by going from stress to serenity, from struggle to satisfaction and from straining to stability.

The word of God says in Romans 15:4... *"for whatsoever things were written before our time, were written for our learning; that we through patience and comfort of the scriptures might have hope."* In the light of that scripture was this book written. You will receive patience, comfort and hope from that which LaTarsha is sharing.

This book conveys this truth: *"The young lions do lack... but they that seek the Lord shall not want any good thing."* It is made clear that as you trust in the Lord you will never lack any good thing. Can you see yourself as a no-lack person: you're not lacking the strength you need or you're not lacking the favor? It is a good thing to know that what you need is in you.

If you don't realize you are enough, then you'll always be dependent on other people to make you feel good about yourself. When you live thinking that you're inadequate, you'll short change yourself, you'll play up to people because that's where you're getting your validation. But when you know you are enough by yourself; you don't rely on people to approve you; you get your approval from God.

LaTarsha helps us to understand that it is a good thing when you understand all of us experience pain; the challenge is, we don't just go through it, we grow through it. Difficulty is an opportunity to get stronger, to develop character, to gain new confidence.

The change that awaits you, as a result of you putting into operation the insight given in reading this book, will truly be beneficial to you and others.

Bishop Roderick Mitchell
The New Life Church Inc.

"I can't believe this is happening to me" or "I don't believe I did that!" I'm sure you've used those phrases, as you have walked through life's trials, twists and turns. Our lives, for the most part, are often shaped by our reactions to those phrases. They leave us feeling shame and broken. Those reactions are

where we allow doubt and fear to rule our lives, our thoughts, and often shape our attitudes.

How we react to those phrases will also determine just how much we "say" we truly trust God. Walking through those "reactions" can make or break you, but God. He reassures us that we are "Still A Good Thing," but we must stand on His Word *"never will I leave you; never will I forsake you."*—**Hebrews 13:5.**

None of our reactions are surprises to God; therefore, we were already equipped to deal with them- not in our strength, but in His; if we allow Him.

Take a moment and remember how you reacted to those phrases. What would you do different? Are you stronger? Are you wiser? Are you at a place in your life where you can even think about it? My sister and first time Author, *LaTarsha Mack* thought about it, through the lens of scripture. Then she became strong enough to talk about it, and then brave enough to write about it. Allow her personal journey to captivate you by her willingness to trust God, her strength to say no to what is not of God and her humility to admit and own her mistakes. She dared to believe who God says she is *"I am fearfully and wonderfully made."*—**Psalm 139:14.**

Transparency is her portion and the pages you are about to read unfolds step-by-step, "her story, her

highs, her lows, and her walk with God." It's not glossy and sugar glazed for your enjoyment—it's real, raw, up close and personal—for your growth and healing. I celebrate Tasha because she engages us in a dialogue that most of us even refuse to acknowledge, because we haven't healed.

Be humble enough, brave enough and strong enough to take an honest look at "you." Know that, like most of us, we may have been broken, but we are "still a good thing." Decide this day to trust God. Healing is here...right here, right now...take it...hold on to it...and don't let go!

Janelle Thompson
Tamarac, Florida

"Life is like a Box of Chocolates"—nothing could be further from the truth.

First, a big "thank you" to my sister, friend, confidant, spiritual advisor and a phenomenal Woman of God, LaTarsha Mack (The real Tasha Mack!)!

LaTarsha, thank you for living as a constant example and validating that all things may not turn out like a box of chocolate, but it can end up much sweeter than it started.

Still A Good Thing

We look for inspiration in those around us and LaTarsha Mack exemplifies exactly that. As you read this personal account of LaTarsha's journey through the 'D' word —divorce, you will better understand that the obstacles you encounter and gain experience from, are your immediate opportunities. Your "slip and fall" decisions will become your "stand strong and don't give up" moments. You will have more useful tools to make it through your next life challenge, getting you closer in completing your purpose on your terms.

Regardless of where you are on your journey, Ms. Mack has provided an excellent account for each of us to review and reflect that we are ABLE. It's up to us to decide, what will become of our ability.

Cathy Curry
Eleuthera, Bahamas

Table of Contents

Introduction

As a little girl, I always loved cartoons and animations. I was such a girly-girl and loved the ideal of a mysterious secret love, forbidden love, and a knight in shining armor, come and rescue me love. So, growing up, I just knew I was going to fall in love, get married, have children and live happily ever after. I was quite mischievous in my own right, and the babysitter of the family.

I was also a dreamer and would make myself fall asleep just so I could dream. Dreaming was my way of escaping from and dealing with reality. Whenever I would dream, I could make whatever I wanted to happen—happen, change it, rearrange it and make the ending be better than the beginning. Needless to say, I loved to sleep; my bed was my comfort zone.

My teenage years were very challenging because I was dealing with discovering me as a young lady, peer pressure, and not having my father around to give me guidance and covering; coming up in a strong Christian family was all I knew. My mother raised five children on her own and I was the third oldest. My father was a good man; however, we grew up most of our lives without him because he was in and out of mental hospitals, as he was diagnosed with the disease of Schizophrenia.[1] I was very close to my father whom I loved and missed immensely. I know for sure, that my siblings also felt the same way.

It never occurred to me that my family was dysfunctional, until I heard *Bishop T.D. Jakes* talk about a dysfunctional family. It was such an *epiphany,* as if a light switch was suddenly flicked on and things became so clear to me. Now that I am older, I am no longer hard on myself, but coming up, I was very hard and critically judgmental of my Christian values.

Every young girl's dream is to one day mature into womanhood and be found by Love.

---

[1] **Schizophrenia** is a mental disorder characterized by abnormal social behavior and failure to understand reality. - www.mayoclinic.org.

I was one of the ones whom wanted to be loved. I gave my all by being transparent and approachable, open and honest. It was easy for me to show how I felt and be expressive. But more than anything, I wanted to be married and have children and for my marriage to be successful, as I don't believe two people ever go into a marriage thinking divorce. I wanted God to be the Head of our marriage and continue to bless our union and guide us through the storms of life together, as we raised our children to reverence and love Him.

Suddenly, all my hopes and dreams were shattered in September, 2001, when my then husband served me a Notice of Divorce. Now walk with me, as I was challenged and pushed to my potential while going through my divorce.

I am often reminded of the scripture, **Proverbs 18:22** which reads, *"He who finds a wife finds a good thing, And obtains favor from the Lord."* Ladies, if you are believing God for a spouse, make sure you are occupied preparing yourself to be his wife: do you know how to cook, how to clean, how to separate laundry and fold the clothes, how to turn your house into a home? By all means necessary, don't wait until

you are found and say, "I do" to learn how to be a wife. No, while you are waiting, become that which you are believing to be.

On April 8, 1995, when my then fiancé and I entered into a covenant union of marriage, I just knew that it could never be broken. The covenant union for me was very important, because the two have now become one. His role as my husband was to cover me and to protect me as his wife. Not every woman is a wife, but I knew that I was one. Take the time to study *Proverbs 31*, it is an example of what we are to become. We were both believers in Christ and we wanted the same things out of life.

We unofficially met in 1993, when my brother was part of a drug program and my mother and I were invited to do a duet at the church that my brother and my ex-husband attended. I will never forget that night because I had just purchased a brand new 1993 Toyota Corolla and after my mother and I finished our duet, Ondarra, my brother, couldn't wait to introduce everyone to us that was a part of the drug program.

I remembered my brother introducing me to everyone except my ex-husband whom I will call 'Tony' that night. But I remembered Tony because he was the most handsome one out of everyone there. We looked at each other from a distance and never said a word; our eyes did all the talking. I liked him from just his appearance, but I never released to anyone what was in my heart on that night.

A year later, Tony saw my mother while shopping and told her, *"tell your daughter that I am looking for my wife."* My mother responded *"I have three daughters and two of them are here with me now."* He rephrased and said to my mother, *"Tell your daughter Tasha that I am looking for my wife;"* my mother gave me his message.

During that period in my life, I was in between jobs, fighting depression, had just lost my apartment and had to move in with my brother and his wife; and yet, I was in the church and serving God with all my heart.

Chapter One
Couples of America

The day Tony and I got married was the happiest day of my life outside of having my children. We were both young and in love, and Tony had a way about him that made me feel like a queen. He was the type of man who sends flowers for every holiday and would surprise me with gifts spontaneously; Oh yes, he spoiled me. Although we both worked, my paycheck was my paycheck and he knew that I would not spend money foolishly.

We always went on family vacations or trips at least twice a year. Our family gatherings and cookouts were always done on a grandiose scale and no one was asked or expected to bring a covered dish, just their appetite. Tony always made sure we had food and all the bills paid. We had our own little system going—whenever we got paid, he would

call me and tell me what bills were to be paid and I would write the checks and drop them in the mail.

Life was just great, our family was centered around Christ; we joined a local church together that had a good amount of young married couples, so we fitted right in. We both became active in our church, I was a Praise and Worship leader, Sunday school teacher and on separate occasions, we would each minister the word whenever the pastor went out of town. The majority of the couples looked up to us because we were a little older than they were. We loved sharing stories on marital highs and lows, how we met and how God delivered us out of predicaments.

We had a good thing going on, until the fishing trip lie; yes, a fishing trip lie. The devil used something so small to destroy our marriage.

My husband at the time worked the night shift, while I worked the day shift. We have three children in which I had the responsibility to get them ready to go to school every day. We had agreed that we would not

put our children into daycare until they were able to talk; so, my husband took care of our youngest son when he came home from working the night shift.

But, this particular morning, he never came home from work as I waited for his arrival. I called him to see what the delay was, I told him, "I need to go to work," but he stated that he would be home shortly something came up at work that required him to stay a little late, and for me to find someone to watch our son until he got home from work.

Needless to say, this placed me in a dilemma because of a last-minute decision in finding someone I could trust to watch our son. I decided to call my job to let them know I would be late so I could wait for my husband's arrival. An hour passed and still no Tony so, I called his phone again to get an update of his arrival, but now I was only getting his voicemail. I then called his office line and was told by the young lady who answered that my husband left the office an hour ago. At first, my mind began to wonder what was going on, as my husband only worked 10 minutes from the house. But now, I am thinking

negatively that something happened to him and I began to worry.

I kept calling and calling, but no answer. So, I decided to call some of his closest friends, but without any success. However, I was still faced with finding someone to watch our son, when I recalled a young lady from the church who kept children out of her home. I called her to ask if she could watch him until I got off from work.

Finally heading to work, I still didn't know what had happened to my husband, so I began to pray and kept calling him and his friends to see if anyone would answer and knew where he was. When I was finally able to connect with one of his friends, to my utter surprise, I was informed that he and several of the men from the church left early that morning to go fishing somewhere in North Florida. For him not to take my job into consideration and finding someone at the last minute to watch our son, while making me believe he was working late, was a LIE just so he could go fishing!

I never thought, as I am writing this, that something such as a lie, would end our marriage. For the most part, many people get divorced for infidelity and financial situations, but a LIE!!!

Now, once the lie was told, everything was set into motion and I stopped talking to him for several weeks. During this time of non-communication, Tony was talking to someone else about his marital problems. This someone else was another young lady and just a few months later, he was moving out of our home. How could this all be happening? This wasn't supposed to be happening to us. Not only was my marriage falling apart, but my home as well. Everything just seemed to stop in time: house in foreclosure, husband gone, and the modest role-model couple was severed. But yet, I continued to press my way into the church sanctuary where I found comfort and where I could praise my way through this test. Not knowing this was going to be one of the most trying tests of my life.

Father, I belong to YOU! All I have, I give to You. Fill me with Your love, surround me with Your Presence! Shalom.

Chapter Two
I'm Such a Fool

There were always good days as long as I wasn't thinking about what I was going through. I could praise God only in the good times, but when the bad times came around, instead of praising, I complained; I glorified the devil and his army. I would wake-up Sunday mornings, get my children and I prepared for service, have a wonderful time in the Lord, leave church, get home and hear something negative that my husband said and I would cry out, *"I'm Such a Fool."*

My husband and I would have long conversations on the phone trying to figure out what we were doing. While I was still trying to convince him that I loved him, and for him to come home so we could work it out, he would still say, *"No, I'm moving on."* And yet, I would cry out, *"I'm Such a Fool!"*

I would call my husband over to the house to talk to him and beg him.... *"please do not do this, I don't want a divorce, look at our children, I don't want another man raising our children."* I would tell him that I loved him, but he would walk away and say, *"No, it is over."* And yet, I would cry out, *"I'm Such a Fool."* I was so vulnerable, desperate and broken, that if my husband had told me to *"stand on one leg and bark like a dog"* I would have eagerly complied. I was such a Fool... Can you relate?

I went through my, *"I'm Such a Fool,"* syndrome for a while. Nothing that I did or said mattered to him anymore. I felt that it was hopeless to even believe God for someone who was so stubborn. My faith in God, walking and talking and even being in His Presence, grew weaker with each passing day. I began to ask God, why? This wasn't supposed to be happening to the Praise and Worship leader. This wasn't supposed to be happening to a minister of the church; No, not me!

I felt like everyone was watching me to see how I would stand under pressure and to see

how well I responded to it. Being that I was one of the leaders of the ministry, everyone was watching to see if I was living by the same words that I had just preached. Many began to talk about me and the way I was handling somethings. I felt like no one knew nor understood the magnitude of the pressure that I was under. All I knew, was that a whole lot of talking was going on and not enough praying. Where were the saints of God when I really needed them; where were they?

Though my faith was weakening, I remember searching for answers in the Word for what I was going through. I was saying, *"I'm Such a Fool"* until I began to believe that no other person on this earth had done the things that I've done and still believed God for their marriage, until I read,

I Corinthians 4:9 (MSG) – *"It seems to me that God has put who bear his Message on stage in a theater in which no one wants to buy a ticket. We're something everyone stands around and stares at, like an accident in the street."*

My life was on display at this point and was like a rollercoaster ride, up and down.

I Corinthians 4:9 began to soothe the sting of being a fool.

Lord, I exalt YOU. You are bigger than the pain I was experiencing. You are Greater than the deepest hurt I ever imagined; please Keep Me!

Chapter Three
Walking in Denial

Growing up in a strong Christian home has always been my strength in everything that I did in life. Whenever I got in trouble or was in a bind, I knew I could go to God and He would work it out and fix it for me. But, as I was faced with divorce, this was one thing I did not believe God could help solve.

I read just about every scripture I could find about divorce. I was really struggling with the acceptance of such a painful cutting away of one's flesh. I would cry nonstop at times, and then I would talk myself right out of depression, and act as if nothing was bothering me; I was like a functioning addict in a dysfunctional role. I was good at faking it until I made it; but I was still dying on the inside. I felt as though God did not hear me and just left me to fix it myself.

Many family members and loved ones gave me scriptures to stand on and to believe God. At times, I was very strong in my faith to believe that whatever I spoke or prayed about, God was going to deliver. But, the more I prayed, it seems the more bad things were happening. It felt like no end and I was not having any peace or rest; many sleepless nights. Not knowing that everything I was going through was in the Plan and Will of God for my life during that particular season.

I remember that in the year 2000, I spoke at a women's conference at the church I attended and the theme for the conference was *Talithacumbe*, meaning damsel arise. The conference had several dynamic speakers and each speaker had something to say about the damsel arising. Before I accepted the invitation for the conference, my marriage and home were a success and we did not have any major storms that year within our marriage and home.

The message I spoke at the conference was, *"Die Damsel Die."* Unbeknownst to me, I was speaking into my own life. A year after speaking at the conference, my home and

marriage began to change and go through a shift that would either make my marriage or break it. Nothing could have prepared me for what I had to endure for the Word sake. I was challenged to the point that change had to happen within me. I had no idea that what I was about to go through would not only bring out the *good* in me, but also the *bad* and the *ugly. You don't know what's in you until you go through. And I often say, in order to get to that place called THERE, you have to go through. Selah.*

One of the bad things the divorce brought out in me, was it caused me to stop trusting God for a moment and start depending on my feelings and emotions; leaning on my own understanding. I was not dealing with rejection well. I could not believe he left me for another woman and had all types of excuses to justify why he was leaving. I just knew the Word of God that was dwelling inside of my husband was going to turn him around and bring him back home. But he was being influenced by others and he had his own agenda and his own mind made up.

When he rejected me, I got angry and started cursing when he made me mad. There were times when I would be loving and kind on the phone with him, and then he would say something the wrong way, and I would just let him have it. Curse words would just begin to form around my mind and I would let them flow right at him. After giving him a piece of my mind, I would come to myself and say, *"Oh God, what is happening to me, I am changing into someone I never thought I would be."*

I could not believe that this thing was bringing the worst out of me. Thank God because anything and everything that was not like God, I wanted out; the cursing was live and in color. All I wanted was my husband and I to work on our marriage and for him to come home. I reacted out of my emotions and I was out of control only when I allowed him to push my buttons. I still had not accepted that he had left and was seeing someone else.

In my mind, we were just going through a phase and the both of us would get over it. I had no idea, while still married to me, my husband was making wedding plans with the

other woman, all while I was still crying out to God, believing Him to restore my marriage.

No matter how I tried to change and to show him that I was changing and that our marriage could work, he made me feel like a fool for trying to save it. It took time and prayer for me to accept the fact that he was really gone this time, and my marriage was over.

In 2003, one year later after my divorce, I was able to start talking about the divorce. I had been looking for jobs outside of my current job to help me to move on from the memories of my husband because at my current job, everyone knew about us.

It was time for a new beginning to get me away from the memories, a new chapter, a fresh start. So, I started looking for a job and finally found one to begin my new life. I did not know that the battle had only just begun. All I wanted was a fresh start in life and for the pain and the wounds to heal. I didn't want any more sleepless nights; but the greatest challenge was within my new job.

With elevation, comes another level of devils and distractions that will try to hinder or stop what God is doing in your life.

Stay Focus!

Chapter Four
Fresh Start

I started my new job as an Administrative Specialist II at a jail facility and it was quite interesting coming from the corporate world to a secure world inside a jail. Not really knowing what to expect, I was clueless of the atmosphere and what the job really entailed. That is usually expected when you transfer into a new career assignment.

I was still trying to get acclimated to my new environment; when I realized that I would be working around a lot of very handsome men. Let me say, it was *"Raining Men."* I had never worked around so many men before, and it was quite challenging being the new kid on the block, as everyone was curious about me. Each day, in addition to having my guard-up, I also had to be prayed-up because I was working in temptation city.

After working there for one week, I was ready to quit because I wasn't used to the attention and all the offers to take me out. Although I was single again, all the rules and games had changed since the last time I dated; I felt like a fish out of water. Trying to have a conversation with a guy wasn't easy because of the pain I still harbored from my divorce. I just wasn't ready to date and I still believed I would not be ready until I was finished working on me.

I'm not going to say that I had not been on dates because I had, but I was not ready for a serious relationship with anyone. At that time, I was lonely and would have loved to have had someone to be a husband to me and a father to my children, but I needed time to deal with me. During that time, I cried many nights asking God, *"What are you doing with me?"*

Have you ever gotten to a place where you don't know what to do and where to go and what steps to take? That is where I was; being broken doesn't feel good at all. It takes you to a place of unfamiliar territory and moves you out of your comfort zone. Realizing the battle is in the mind, I was still learning to breathe

again, in order to get a fresh start on life. At times, I felt like I was not moving or going anywhere, but I knew I was still on the Potter's wheel going through my purging process.

It was during this time in my life that I was ready to be still and allow God to rearrange me. God was putting in and taking out what was needed and necessary for this journey.

Praise Break:

Romans 8:26-28MSG says, *"Meanwhile, the moment we get tired in the waiting, God's Spirit is right alongside helping us along. If we don't know how or what to pray, it doesn't matter. He does our praying in and for us, making prayer out of our wordless sighs, our aching groans. He knows us far better than we know ourselves, knows our pregnant condition, and keeps us present before God. That's why we can be so sure that every detail in our lives of love for God is worked into something good."* Hallelujah Glory to God!

Keep in mind, the *Battle Continues...*

Chapter Five
The Battle Continues

June 2005, would have been three years since the divorce, but the memories seemed like yesterday. I had been dating for 8 months and the relationship was very stressful, but *addicting to say the least*. To be perfectly honest, he wasn't a Christian; he didn't believe in God at all. The scripture says, *"how can two walk together unless they agree?"*

I constantly asked myself, what was I doing in this relationship? Here's the Answer: *"my flesh was being sexually fulfilled, satisfied and entertained; I was completely absorbed in the sin of lust."* In this case, my reward was sex.

Have you ever been lured *(... to do something or to go somewhere, especially by offering some form of reward)*[2] and lay in the

---

[2] www.dictionary.com

bed of self-condemnation? My natural needs were being met, but my spiritual needs were not. I suddenly had a revelation of what Paul meant when he said, *"that which I shouldn't do, I do and that which I should do, I don't."*

If you answered Yes to the above scenario, meditate on the below scripture:

Romans 8:1-2 *says, "There is therefore now no condemnation to those who are in Christ Jesus, who do not walk according to the flesh, but according to the Spirit. For the law of the Spirit of life in Christ Jesus has made me free from the law of sin and death."*

I Now give you permission to Forgive yourself from all condemnation and be FREE in Jesus Name!

I was in limbo with my faith in God, I was compromising with the devil, but yet, my spirit man was crying out for Help! I was acting out of the pain and rejection that I was still dealing with from the divorce. God, Please Help Me!

However, in the meantime, a void was being filled with a filler. A filler (in my definition), is something or someone that

replaces or fill-in an empty space. I was ok with the filler because he made me feel good, he made me feel like a woman, he fulfilled my every sexual desire. (I will expound more on the Filler in Chapter Seven.)

Now ladies, it is not about our feelings. I was struggling to break away from the feelings and the emotional attachment of the filler because I knew better, but the devil had me believing that I couldn't get out or away from him. I have learned that when we give into our feelings and open the door to sin no matter what it is, we give the devil access and authority to lure us back to his domain.

"BUT I had a Praying Mother!"

After being faithful in the church for so many years, praying, believing, fasting, and ministering to so many people, I was spiritually burned out. Now, I was at a crossroad in my walk with God; I was still acting out the pain, the hurt, and the disappointments. I often asked myself, *"Where is God? Why did this have to happen to me?"* But I was constantly reminded of all the women before me that had to go through

the fire to come out as pure gold. Did I still have a fight in me?

Though there is pleasure in sin; it will eventually lead to death and a permanent separation from God; hence why we must fight and bind the strongman. I know the battle is in my mind, and the constant struggle to be who God called me to be, but I was being distracted, listening to others telling me what they believed God had called me to be. I was at the place where God needed my full attention; I was ready, willing and yearning to hear His Voice. I needed to fight the spirit of distraction that the devil was using against me. We must resolve within that our life is not our own; we belong to Jesus.

Trying to put the past behind me and move forward, made it difficult for me to trust ministries anymore. Knowing that God had a call on my life, I knew I needed to get back into the things of God, but where should I go, where should I start and who would be my Shepherd? This was very important to me because I needed to be taught and ministered to. *"I finally realized that adversity, it really*

doesn't matter."—*Apostle Dr. John H. Chambers.*

Remember me God, your daughter LaTarsha; I have the mind of Christ. Teach me your ways Oh Lord, that I may obey your word. Nevertheless, not my will, but thy will be done in my life. In Jesus Name. Amen.

Chapter Six
God Come Chase Me

Being in this relationship was putting a strain on me both emotionally and physically. At times, I still couldn't see my way out. I knew he wasn't a God-fearing man, but I wanted it to work. Come on ladies, some of you know what I am talking about; You settled! That's exactly what I was doing. However, in my spirit, I knew it was wrong and God Himself was making it hard for us no matter what we tried to do.

In my quiet times alone with God, I would just lay in my bed and Worship Him. I had gotten to a point where I couldn't pray words anymore; I just Worshipped Him because I knew He understood me. But in the middle of my worship, I said, *"God, Come Chase Me."* I wanted Him to come and get me because I couldn't bring myself to where He was. I'm reminded of the Word of God that

reads, *"For whom the Lord loveth he chasteneth, and scourgeth every son whom he receiveth."*—**Hebrews 12:6.**

I knew within myself I had to intentionally cry out for God to come help me. I am learning in this walk of life that no matter what state of mind you are in; God is still Faithful and Just. He loves us enough to come see about us when we are in places we shouldn't be and doing things we shouldn't be doing. He still has a word for you and He still has need of you.

Now, I am not suggesting to wallow in your sin, you must fight your way out. Sin has a way of looking good, feeling good and being fulfilling; but it's only for a season; and the end therein is death. **—Read Proverbs 16:25.**

So, I fought, I knew very well, that I couldn't do this on my own. It was time for me to be transparent with God and man, so I called on the elders to pray for me because I was weak. Though I enjoyed the pleasure that came with the sin, the sin was a heavy weight that was wearing me down, but I was determined to please God. However, at first,

I believed the lie, that I couldn't come out of this sinful revolving door mess.

One day, my guy friend opened his mouth and said the "L-word." Now, I just told you I was struggling to get free and here he comes with "I Love You" pulling on my vulnerability and emotional heart strings. I responded by saying "please don't say the L-word." Suddenly, God told me how to respond to my guy friend. God gave me the desire to live Holy and Righteous. The words He gave me to speak outwardly into the atmosphere were, "I love God more than sin." When I said those words, something on the inside shook my soul and the chains were broken. Won't He Do It!

Chapter Seven
Torn Between Two Lovers

In hindsight, I knew the moment when I went out on the first date with him that he wasn't the one. Why did I compromise; why did I entertain him, why did I engage in the conversation, why did I subject myself to this type of relationship? I now understand that it was purely self-gratification. I was doing those things that were pleasing to my flesh.

My spirit man was crying out for me to do that which was right, the entire time. The more I fed my flesh, the hungrier it became, but in that hunger, my spirit man was still fighting for me. I knew in my spirit that I had to let it go and get back to the things of God. But I had to have a made-up mind and my heart had to be fixed on doing the things of God.

That relationship was a distraction, but I couldn't see it at the time. He was a loving and kind man, but yet, controlling. He had to be the center of my attention and my only focus, thus God came after meeting his needs; I couldn't go on with it. I began to remember what God had done for me and my children, and what He had brought us out of and I knew I had to end it.

Even though I knew I had to get out of this relationship, the soul tie made it a struggle to let go; I was torn between two lovers. Christ was my lover and I loved Him, and I knew Christ loved me with a perfect love, but my flesh would not let go of the man, the "Filler."

When I think about what mattered most and who loved me the most, I was reminded of how Jesus loved me so much that He gave His life for me to live; how He suffered and was afflicted so I may be healed; how He loved me, yet while I was sinning and continued to love me right out of my sins. How then, could I be in love with God, and the devil (who is the enemy of God)?

I have come to the conclusion that if they don't have the Spirit of Christ, they are anti-Christ. They are persuaded by the devil and will do whatever he tells them to do. An enemy of Christ is an enemy of mine. So, if I continued to sow to my flesh, I will reap nothing but the flesh, but if I sow to the Spirit, then I will gain spiritual things, and that is where the battle is to this day—*flesh vs. spirit.*

He agreed to attend church with me, and even sit with me, but nevertheless asked that I not tell anyone that he didn't believe in God. That was how badly he wanted to be with me, but he still wouldn't believe that this 'God stuff' is real. I was told that I can go to church every other Sunday and maybe one night a week, but the rest of my time had to be centered and focused around him. All of that, just to have a relationship with someone who wasn't my husband.

Now, I am sharing what really happened to me. I am not ashamed to expose myself and what I went through to become free, in order to help other women to also become free; this battle was between the flesh and the spirit. My

flesh wanted to continue in sin, but my spirit man was battling for me. I wasn't going through this alone, I had my covenant sisters in Christ, who understood the struggles I was facing and were interceding for me.

It was crucial that I started writing how I truly felt about this relationship and why I convinced myself that he was the ideal man. What I was desiring was commitment, someone who was in tuned with me and wanted to get to know me on an intimate level without becoming physical. After watching the movie: *"Mr. Wright"* with *"Queen Latifah,"* it really inspired me not to settle. I knew I was 'Ms. **R**ight' and I was working on my profile to meet 'Mr. Wright.'

I realized that I was getting older, as were my children and I really didn't want to be by myself. I wanted someone who made me laugh and was very affectionate. I am into sports, and I wanted to be able to let my hair down and just be me.

The most important thing I desired, was for him to be my friend, where we could just talk and be open about anything without being

critical and judgmental. My life was pretty complex with me being a single parent and going to school, I wanted to be able to enjoy life full circle, but yet, be able to spend quality time with my man and children.

I wanted to be able to go on long vacations and romantic rendezvous and be able to worship the Lord within the same household; I wanted to experience a joyful and successful relationship. I welcome and embrace challenges and changes that will elevate our relationship to the next level.

I have learned by listening to other women who have experienced relationship meltdowns, to be specific to God in your prayers about what type of man you would like. I always felt that this was unnecessary until I started being a magnet that attracted the guys that were needy and required their egos to be inflated and massaged.

So, I started denouncing all soul ties of past relationships and began to declare and decree what I wanted in a man.

A man of faith, courage and strength, financially stable and able to go beyond the limits (whatever that may be).

A man in his right now, but still adventurous and willing to take risks, not afraid of challenges and looks adversities straight in the eye.

A man confident in himself, but yet, warm, welcoming, inviting and able to hold a conversation without being intimidated or intimidating, be a confident leader in his role as a man, husband and father to my children.

A man, able to make good sound decisions and judgments and who is confident in the decisions he has made. Be the protector and able to make provisions without struggling and complaining.

A man, who will treat me with love, honor and respect; as his QUEEN! Love my children as his own and has God as the Head of his life.

Chapter Eight
Dealing with Self

I finally realized that I had to deal with self. No more hiding behind the mask. It was time to take off the mask and face the woman in the mirror. For years, I lived under everyone's shadow and did not attend to what mattered to me the most. I was everyone's personal cheerleader and their mediator; I had no identity.

I didn't know what I wanted or where I wanted to go in life, but what I did know was that destiny was calling me; there was something deep within that I knew I had to do for ME! I no longer waited for the approvals of peers and family members. I knew, as the righteousness of Christ, clothed in His Glory, I was already approved by God.

As I continued to change, I knew that God was with me. If my family members had not been praying for me and if I did not KNOW

that God was with me, I would have lost my mind several times over. My frustration caused me to constantly ask God "WHY?"

Why me; why all of the pain and the hurt, why the divorce, you know the 'Oh why me syndrome.' Then I began to change my speech by saying, why not me? It's obvious that God knew all this was going to happen and He is now getting the Glory out of my life through my pain and discomfort; life is to be altered for the Glory of God. He is restoring and rebuilding my life for His Purpose.

When we know the Word of God, our lives should be governed by it. I am often pondering on why we do some of the things we do when we should know better, right!

Then of course, I remember Apostle Paul in his writing: *"The things I should do, I don't and the things I shouldn't do, I do."* This serves as a reminder, that we will be constantly battling in the mind and flesh until we learn to put it under subjection by the Word of God. It sounds like a quick solution when in essence, it's not easily done if there is a

stronghold in operation. The battle is constantly in the mind, but we have to have a made-up mind to want to fight that which has held us captive to sin.

Sisters, trust me, I have already walked out the steps you are now taking, making decisions in the heat of the moment and dealing with the consequences. Yet, you are tormented in your mind because the battlefield is in the mind, warring between reality and your faith that God will change the situation and bring deliverance.

To go against the grain of my faith, emotions, expectations, failures, uncertainties and to constantly be reminded that my children were watching my every move. They were monitoring how I act, how I handled each crisis, and every situation because I was their example. I was teaching them how to react and respond to unexpected storms, and catastrophic situations that will reveal weakness, strength, and fears.

However, the moment of decision will also reveal when I was pulled from out of my comfort zone and forced to face the reality of

the here and now. Dealing with sleepless nights, battling depression, not being able eat properly because my nervous system was being tampered with, and my emotions and anxiety weighted heavily upon me.

Knowing that the one you loved and understanding that this relationship was suddenly over, moves me with tears of compassion for him as his inner pains and demons; but compassion for his sickness is not enough. You had to endure enough pain and misery and not allow your emotions to give in or be tricked into believing he is sorrowful for the wrong he has imparted unto the family.

Although I know your heart reaches out to his heart to help it beat the same rhythm, you have to continue to believe that both of you win against the evil plot of the devil. But it goes beyond your expectations, you must give up that which you love as a sacrifice unto God and allow Him to place a ram in the bush for you.

Ladies, I feel your pain, your silent frustration, and the tug of war in your

emotions and the constant battle in the mind. It's kind of hard to direct all the negative energy to God, so He may take it away from you to allow peace and rest to reign over you. While you ponder on how and why He allowed this to happen, and the years of investment, now coming to an end, remember you are the one that were and are still willing to fight for it.

You just need to be reassured that it is worth the fight because you are tired of the embarrassment, negligence, and most importantly, out of it all, the "RESPECT." You are the Favor God bestowed unto a man when he finds you because you are the *"GOOD THING."*

Chapter Nine
Getting Self Out of the Equation

I finally understood that nothing can be solved if you don't know what the problem is. You must first identify the problem and then come up with a solution. I realized I could not do anything without Christ. Therefore, I chose to remove myself from the equation, and place God in it, and allow Him to make it right.

An equation would not be an equation without having a solution. When life brings up challenging situations, we must allow the Holy Spirit to show us how to resolve them. If you listen to the Holy Spirit, He will show you the right way.

I never thought in a thousand years, that my ex-husband and I, would have been able to have an amicable relationship. I had to remove 'self' from the equation and replace 'self' with God. Once I did that, I was able to

see through the eyes of God how to handle our previous disagreements. This was a learning experience!

This experience was for me to totally submit and surrender everything to God. I had to live out all of **James 4:7,** *"Submit yourselves therefore to God, resist the devil and he will flee from you."* I was struggling, and it appeared that the struggle had power and authority over me.

Everything I thought I knew, and how to make it work couldn't explain how I was acting nor feeling; I needed God to show me the way. I began to *submit* my will to Him by yielding all that I am and all that I have to Him. I began to Trust God again, so the healing could begin. I was like an onion being peeled, one layer at a time yet, crying with every peel in order to get closer to the Will of God for my life and to reside in His Presence. I no longer needed or wanted to hide behind the mask of hurt, pain and disappointment.

The mask, now shattered, and the girl that once lived inside the box of shame, hurt, pain, defeat, anger, and disappointment has come

alive, and now able to confront it all to destroy the box that once held her prisoner.

Suddenly, everything changed, and nothing remained the same; Everything changed for **ME**.

Chapter Ten
Now is My Time Outside of the Box

ast night, I heard the Spirit of God say, *"It's time to come back to the fold."* Now the definition of fold is: *a flock of sheep; a group of people united by a common faith: a church and its members.*[3] Meaning, coming from a distant place, a place where you don't know where you are and don't know what to do, and you are just out there, but you spread your wings and fly back into His Presence to a closed position where you are seated at His feet, nourishing from the residue of His Glory surrounding you.

Looking at how successful the world is without inviting God into their affairs makes me upset with how it continues to prosper. With so many setbacks because of the divorce, now is my time to prosper, flourish,

---

[3] www.merriam-webster.com.

and grow. No longer will I be inside the box; I am determined to rise and destroy the box.

It was the beginning of dawn on a Saturday, and my dream of doing a photoshoot was about to begin. It was all about me, the *woman,* I had become, to the *woman,* I am *destined* to be. For once, I wasn't living in my comfort zone (inside the box), I was finally living outside the box and beyond its boundaries.

It was time for me to accomplish another goal and leave a legacy behind for my children and those whose lives I would impact. It all started with me reclaiming my self-worth and seeing myself through God's eyes.

Although it was a little after dawn, it was still dark, but the sun was set to rise within minutes, as we prepared for the photoshoot. The ocean was calm and still, but I had an eerie feeling, and my mind was racing with fear of the unknown. I felt fear beginning to overwhelm me, and what should have been a peaceful ocean view seemed instead to be a menacing scene from the "Walking Dead."

I turned to my daughter and said, *"I'm not sure if I can do this."* I didn't know how to swim and I didn't know what was about to happen, as to how the shoot would go. I also didn't believe I could be expressive enough to show the real me while being in an unfamiliar place. I knew I wanted to express myself by letting go, and being free from worries, fears, heartaches and pain; this was something I knew I needed to do. But because of my fear, my perception was distorted and what should have been a tranquil, beautiful scene instead seemed more like a nightmare, the total opposite of what it should have been.

I patiently waited for the photographer's instructions and paid close attention to every word he was saying to make this photoshoot a success. Inside, I felt like a scared little girl because others will now become a part of my world and my life experiences whether good or bad. I was puzzled because this was a new experience for me and a different language all together. I was eager to learn and yet be expressive, as I began to set the stage of my life's journey to freedom.

Being confident in my own skin, I wanted women all over the world to be free like me. Free from worry about how we look, if we're too fat or the blemishes we have on our skin (i.e. stretch marks, scars). I wanted them to experience the beauty that's on the inside that would supersede the outside. That is why I was so glad the photographer understood my story that I was telling. No longer was I to look like the girl next door or the model in the magazine; I was being me, sexy, beautiful, and confident.

During each photoshoot session, I envisioned myself being placed in the center stage of a crowd of people yearning to hear what I had to say. I wanted to be humble, meek and compassionate with everyone so they would understand my story. Throughout the photoshoot, I wanted each picture to represent the woman I am today; the woman I am destined to be. I am ready to fulfill this new chapter in my life, with my greatest accomplishments and successes.

I believed that there were no more chains holding me bound. It was an exhilarating experience facing the fear of the ocean that had

crippled me earlier on; although I was still conscious of the eerie feeling I had before I started the photoshoot. I remember when I was 25, a young man shared with me the revelation of the word FEAR: "False Evidence Appearing Real."

Standing in the warm ocean was empowering, it increased my confidence level to high, an experience of a lifetime, and I wanted to relish every moment and to make a mark right there and say to the world, this is me, this is who I am. Although I have some wounds, let me show you my scars, let me share with you my experience, let me compel you to dare to be you. Allow me to show you that you can overcome anything!

With my emotions already running high and cameras focused on me, I realized in a moment how superstars must feel, having the cameras constantly on them. Every pose, every position, every emotion on my face told a story. I wondered if the audience could look into my eyes and experience the depths of my pain, despair, uncertainty, the emotional rollercoaster and finally, beauty for ashes.

Being outside the box felt great, I was in tuned with myself, my life, and my self-worth. Although trials do come, I'm reminded that they come to make you stronger. I am now stronger, wiser, and I am going beyond my expectations; tackling my fears.

The storm is over and I can see clearly now; my future looks brighter every day. No more living inside the box where I was clothed in darkness, surrounded by fear and controlled by my emotions. Imagine coming out of the box, our comfort zone or state of complacency. You can now reach beyond where your arms can stretch and see beyond where your eyes can see.

Will you capture the moment and step outside the comfort of your limitations?

We are often guided by pejorative advice of others who may not want to see us succeed. We then take hold of the negative words that have permeated our mind and soul and start to believe them; stinking thinking.

I would have never gotten out of my box if I hadn't changed the way I saw myself. I had to believe in me even though there was a lot of

negative energy surrounding me. I had to fight my way out of it by believing and expecting greater than my wildest dreams. Once I let go and got out of the box, I began to experience the fullness of life, it was like breaking away not for just the moment; but for eternity. Look at me Now!

It's not good enough to just live outside the box; it is best to live beyond it. Because, when we step outside of the box, but keep the box within reach, we might still be tempted to go back; as we tend to use the box as a crutch or security blanket. I challenge everyone to destroy the box that has held you captive for so many years; begin to live beyond your wildest dreams; learn to *"Believe Bigger"* – *Marshawn Evans Daniels.*

Chapter Eleven
I Just Got to Be Me

I just learned how to solve riddles yesterday while visiting my sister Angie. Her girls were playing a game to solve riddles, but it is very hard trying to solve a riddle when you are clueless to the facts, however, once you have the facts, it's easy to solve. That's it! Something so simple can be so complicated without the right information.

Playing this game of riddles sparked something deep within me; an Epiphany[4]. The year was 2009, and I began to think about my life and the many phases I had gone through. I was 42, a divorcee, and struggling with what "*I coined the Self-Syndrome*" -- self-centered, self-confidence, self-destruction, self-esteem,

---

[4] It was a Supernatural Sudden Encounter with *I AM.*

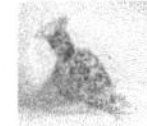

self-love, self-pity, self-respect, self-worth; basically, I was beyond toxic.

Suddenly, I realized *"I Just Got to Be Me."* "What do you mean? I am glad you asked." No more living in someone else's shadow; it was time to take control of my life, my emotions, my purpose, my destiny and begin to restore my relationship with a covenant Father to become the woman He preordained for me to be; not who I am, but whose I AM— it was time to become authentically me. With that revelation, my failed marriage no longer had a hold on me.

In the blink of an eye, I reclaimed my life and took dominion and walked into my truth and freedom. In order for us to be who God called us to be, we must die to the "Self-Syndrome" and replace it with the Great I AM, that I AM.

Philippians 2:5(AMP)— *"Have this same attitude in yourselves which was in Christ Jesus (look to Him as your example in selfless humility).*

But God!

When the challenges of life show up uninvited and unexpected, and it will, we must remember that our God is still in control and nothing that happens to us will ever catch Him off guard.

God strategically created and designed me for whatever reason to "FIT —— Fight It Through!" That's right, never giving up and having no other way, but to pull myself up and out of the depts of defeat while looking victory right in the eye and placing it upon my shoulders.

When I occasionally allow myself to reflect back on our plight with nearly becoming homeless, having lost everything except the very *ruach* or breath of God that kept me alive, to fight again, and again, no matter where I am at, I can suddenly become undignified in radical praise to Jehovah. Hallelujah!

The support I desperately needed showed up by way of my mother, sisters and brothers and without reservation, I swallowed by pride and accepted their assistance. "It takes a village to raise a family."

But I was so grateful to God because in the month of April, 2009, I almost lost my life when I was rushed to the hospital with severe chest pains.

It was agenda Thursday at the City of Fort Lauderdale, where I worked, and we were all trying to complete the process of approving agendas. During the day, I started having several chest pains that would go away gradually and then return; but I thought it was just heart burn.

As the day progressed, I noticed the pain was lasting longer, but it was still bearable until I felt like someone pulled my heart out of my chest and was squeezing it, until it stopped moving. That was when I knew something was wrong and I quickly asked my boss to call 911.

When the EMT arrived, they immediately began to treat me, as if I was having a heart attack. They asked me several medical questions and I answered accordingly. All the while, I was praying within my mind and spirit that I should live and not die; while thinking of my children and how much they needed me. I was also saying within myself that I am

too young for this to be happening. When I arrived at the hospital's emergency room, they immediately took me in the back and began to run several tests on me; EKG, chest x-rays and a CAT scan.

While waiting in the room for the test results, family, friends, co-workers were all praying for me. The doctor came into the room with my results and explained that I had two blood clots on my lungs (pulmonary embolism or "PE") and that I was being admitting into the hospital; needless to say, I was not happy. I was confused, I thought I was going to get a shot of medicine and be released, but that didn't happen!

The doctor explained that if the blood clots travelled, they could burst and I would die; I realized how close I came to death. But, although the pain was constant, I had a peace within, that all was well with me.

The 4 days I spent in the hospital gave me time to speak with GOD and reflect on my life. I had so many questions for Him, and I wanted Him to answer them ALL. I thought about the recent relationship that I was in, and

how it wasn't good for me; I thought about what I could do to not allow what happened in previous relationships, to stop me from moving on to new and better committed relationships and possible marriage.

The key to all of this was first being true to myself and being me. No longer did I want to walk in anyone's shadow or their opinion of what a relationship is or should be. I just wanted someone to love me, understand me, grow with me, share my dreams and aspirations, help raise my children and live happily ever after. Thinking to myself, this wasn't easy, it was quite complicated, but it can be done.

Yes, I am a believer and I was once faithful to the "CROSS," but because of my first failed marriage and church hurt, I never really got back into the things of God. I was struggling with my faith walk with God and was barely hanging on by a string.

Although I knew God had a call on my life, I was complacent to do nothing in church. I was content being the soccer mom, going to school and work. Success to me was being free

of people and what they thought of me and doing whatever made me happy.

I knew God existed and I have felt HIS Presence, but I no longer wanted to get involved with the day-to-day activities in church; I just wanted to go to church, hear the sermon and go home. Still, a part of me was missing the worship, the relationship and the conversation with the FATHER. I was missing the interaction of ministering to God's people through my singing of worship and leading people into HIS Presence. Oh, how I truly missed it but, there it goes again the big ole "BUT" that kept getting in the way of my decisions to follow through with what I knew was the right thing to do; forgetting about myself and concentrating on HIM, and worship.

I had to constantly remind myself that my life is not my own. Although I just had to be me, it really wasn't about me. It was about God and His Kingdom, and the position God had me in. It was all in God's timing, and I believe this was His way of getting my attention.

"Lord, keep me as the apple of your eye; hide me in the shadow of your wings." **(Psalms 17:8).** No more me, but more of You, Lord!

Chapter Twelve
The "BUT" Syndrome

For some reason we all have to deal with the "BUT's" in our lives. I usually tell my kids, anything after "BUT" is a lie. This was my way of making them face whatever they needed to face head on without hesitation. At times, when we are dealing with making decisions, our initial thought or instinct tells us what to do and that is usually the right thing to do.

The moment we hesitate and begin to second guest ourselves and to rationalize our decisions, we have gone to another level in our thought process, and we may end up making the wrong decision. On the spiritual aspect of it, we should seek God in all things and trust that HE will lead us and guide us by the Holy Spirit.

Because I hadn't been spending quality time with the God, my spiritual ears were a bit

dull and hearing from Heaven was like listening for a needle to drop in a hay stack. My spirit man was weak due to the lack of word power (meaning not reading and meditating on God's word).

I knew I had to return back to my first love, believing, knowing and trusting that God's Word is true. I had to fight the distractions and the excuses of getting back into the Word of God. In this dispensation of time, we must fight through the distractions; because in distraction we lose focus and valuable time.

In the Kingdom of God, there is no downtime nor spare time, we must always be ready because the devil is seeking whom he may devour. He would rather that we waste time or spend time doing something else rather than investing in building up ourselves to show ourselves approved.

Although life threw me a bag of sour lemons, I was determined to make good sweet lemonade. I started believing again and allowing my friend patience, to have her

perfect work in me. *James 1:4-8*, is the scripture where I began *Faithing It.*

Father God, I'm nothing without you. I come to you asking for forgiveness of not trusting you and waiting on you. I will allow You to be God and Lord of and over my Life. Amen.

Chapter Thirteen
Be Ye Transformed

Everything in life is about choices, and I believe God allowed everything on this journey to happen so His purpose could be revealed and fulfilled in my life.

God is Strategic. He will use everything, every good and bad decision we make, He will turn it around and use it for our good and His Glory to be revealed and at the appointed time.

Romans 8:28(AMP) *"And we know (with great confidence) that God (who is deeply concerned about us) causes all things to work together (as a plan) for good for those who love God, to those who are called according to His plan and purpose."*

Here's a prime example. The plan I had for the release of this book was the summer of 2018. However, life happened and

Still A Good Thing laid dormant within the birthing canal until the end of 2019. But you are reading it at the appointed time; thereby it was not One Day Late!

God is All Knowing, but we must be aligned with His word and His will for our lives. For instance, when we are having sleepless nights from stress and worry, we are not trusting Him. He is waiting for us to totally trust and depend on Him. But this is a process that requires daily transformation by renewing the mind so that we will be able to overcome every hurt, pain, disappointment and resentment that the enemy uses to keep us captive and a slave to sin.

It is my sincere desire, that after reading this book, you will come to Yourself, tell Self, that YOU don't belong to Yourself. You belong to GOD and all He wants is a *"YESS—Yield, Everything, Submit and Surrender."* It's time to make the WORD of GOD first place and the final Authority over EVERYTHING. So, change your mind and replace it with the mind of Christ!

When we take His mind, we will think like Him, look like Him, see like Him, love like Him, give like Him, serve like Him but most importantly when we allow God to totally transform us, and we become one with Christ, then, the world will see Him in us.

So, I changed my MIND and replaced it with GOD! You can do it to. It's called RENEWING the Mind by daily reading the Word of God, having a RELATIONSHIP and FELLOWSHIP with HIM! I now walk in the rhythm of God's word and I agree with HIM.

Romans 12:1-2(AMPC)

"I APPEAL to you therefore, brethren, and beg of you in view of [all] the mercies of God, to make a decisive dedication of your bodies [presenting all your members and faculties] as a living sacrifice, holy (devoted, consecrated) and well pleasing to God, which is your reasonable (rational, intelligent) service and spiritual worship.

Do not be conformed to this world (this age), [fashioned after and adapted to its external, superficial customs], but be transformed (changed) by the [entire] renewal of your mind

[by its new ideals and its new attitude], so that you may prove [for yourselves] what is the good and acceptable and perfect will of God, even the thing which is good and acceptable and perfect [in His sight for you]."

It's time to change and Be Ye Transformed!

Chapter Fourteen
Just Be God

Ever thought about the stop, drop and roll process of putting out a fire? The person who is on fire is confused, disoriented, as not only are they on fire, but they are also in the midst of a fire. The same concept of stop, drop and roll can be applied to getting your "Praise On." Because "Praise" is a weapon against the enemy and gets your attention off of your issues and onto GOD.

Although you are on fire or in the midst of it, think about the three Hebrews boys, *Shadrach, Meshach and Abednego.* While the heat is turned on and up 7 times hotter, turn your "Praise On" and up 7 times hotter and watch "GOD" move in the midst of it. So, stop and drop all your worries and cares, and rollout the "PRAISES"!

Wow, what a difference the "Word of God" makes. Here is something to encourage and empower you to keep the FAITH!

2 Cor. 9:8 *"And God is able to make all grace abound toward you; that ye,* **always** *having* **all** *sufficiency in* **all** *things, may abound to every good work."*

So why are you worrying about anything? God does not want us to worry about our right now, our tomorrow, our soon to come, nor the future. He wants us to acknowledge Him in everything we do. "His GRACE" is sufficient!

He said we always have sufficiency in all things, just think about that for a minute! You'll Give God some Praise! The Word of God says, *"He's sufficient in all things"* so, if you are experiencing lack, then check your walk, your talk, and your giving because no Child of God should be experiencing nor operating in lack.

And remember, that even in the midst of what the world is calling an *"Economic Meltdown;"* He is all Sufficient!

For God to be God in our lives, we must let go of the reigns and our will, and "LET" God be God. We need to go back to the basics of making Him first place and our final authority over everything. *Jeremiah 29:11,* is the blue print for all believers; being God in our lives requires US, YOU, WE to do something and that is to call upon Him, go Pray, and Seek His Face.

No more distractions, no more excuses. God requires us to give Him our all, withholding nothing.

We have to become all of **Philippians 2:5—** *"Let this mind be in you, which was also in Christ Jesus."*

Then we have to become **Romans 8:14—** *"For as many as are led by the Spirit of God, they are the sons of God."*

Then we need to continue to build, **Jude 1:20-21 (MSG)—** *"But you, dear friends, carefully build yourselves up in this most holy faith by praying in the Holy Spirit, staying right at the center of God's love, keeping your arms open and outstretched, ready for the mercy of*

our Master, Jesus Christ. This is the unending life, the real life!"

GOD, it all belongs to YOU!

About the Author

Minister LaTarsha Mack debuts into the literary arena with "Still A Good Thing (Damaged BUT not Undone)" and takes you on an intimate journey of revealing the real and emotional rawness of the unexpected road name 'divorce.'

Minister Mack is a woman fervently pursuing the heartbeat of God and in doing so, wears many hats. She's currently the Administrator for her church, *"Believers of Authority Ministry"* under the leadership of Apostle, Dr. John H. Chambers, and she's a council leader for the *Women of Excellence Ministry*.

The hat she's most proud of wearing is being a mother to Jamea, Jalil and Josiah. Minister Mack walks in the authority to bring change and to help others to walk and talk right into destiny, to speak into existence what God says and be an enemy to failure, defeat, and give up. Work the word, so the Word of God can effectually work in You—that belief is her daily motto.

An entrepreneur, multi-marketing consultant, mentor and a motivational speaker, Minister Mack is passionate about sharing her Christian life, living in the combat zone and walking in victory every day. She keeps it real by identifying the, who's, what's, when's, where's, and how's to prepare for battle so you can be victorious on this Christian walk.

She is the founder of We Believe God Prayer and Devotional line that is changing lives all over

the world. With early morning devotions, she encourages daily living and daily transformation by reading the Word of God and having a relationship and God's mind set to exemplify Christ in the world. The founder of the *Proverbs 31 Woman Empowerment Group* that seeks to lead women into a personal relationship with Christ. With *Proverbs 31:10-31* as a guide, *Proverbs 31 Woman Empowerment Group* reaches women in the middle of their busy days through free devotions, podcasts, speaking events, and conferences.

We are real women offering real-life solutions to those striving to maintain life's balance, in spite of today's hectic pace and cultural pull away from godly principles. Wherever a woman may be on her spiritual journey, *Proverbs 31 Woman Empowerment Group* exists to be a trusted friend who understands the challenges she faces, walks by her side, encouraging her as she walks toward the Heart of God.